Rick's Carrot

Rick is hungry, but his carrot has disappeared! Who has taken it? Come along

This picture book targets the /r/ sound and is part of *Speech Bubbles 2*, a series of picture books that target specific speech sounds within the story.

The series can be used for children receiving speech therapy, for children who have a speech sound delay/disorder, or simply as an activity for children's speech sound development and/or phonological awareness. They are ideal for use by parents, teachers or caregivers.

Bright pictures and a fun story create an engaging activity perfect for sound awareness.

Picture books are sold individually, or in a pack. There are currently two packs available – *Speech Bubbles 1* and *Speech Bubbles 2.* Please see further titles in the series for stories targeting other speech sounds.

Melissa Palmer is a Speech Language Therapist. She worked for the Ministry of Education, Special Education in New Zealand from 2008 to 2013, with children aged primarily between 2 and 8 years of age. She also completed a diploma in children's writing in 2009, studying under author Janice Marriott, through the New Zealand Business Institute. Melissa has a passion for articulation and phonology, as well as writing and art, and has combined these two loves to create *Speech Bubbles*.

What's in the pack?

User Guide

Vinnie the Dove

Rick's Carrot

Harry the Hopper

Have You Ever Met a Yeti?

Zack the Buzzy Bee

Asher the Thresher Shark

Catch That Chicken!

Will the Wolf

Magic Licking Lollipops

Jasper the Badger

Platypus and Fly

The Dragon Drawing War

Rick's Carrot

Targeting the /r/ Sound

Melissa Palmer

Routledge
Taylor & Francis Group

LONDON AND NEW YORK

First published 2021
by Routledge
2 Park Square, Milton Park, Abingdon, Oxon OX14 4RN

and by Routledge
52 Vanderbilt Avenue, New York, NY 10017

Routledge is an imprint of the Taylor & Francis Group, an informa business

British Library Cataloguing-in-Publication Data
A catalogue record for this book is available from the British Library

Library of Congress Cataloging-in-Publication Data
A catalog record has been requested for this book

ISBN: 978-1-138-59784-6 (set)
ISBN: 978-0-367-64853-4 (pbk)
ISBN: 978-1-003-12658-4 (ebk)

Typeset in Calibri
by Newgen Publishing UK

Rick's Carrot

Rick the **r**abbit was **r**eally hungry. He was **r**eally looking forward to eating his **r**ipe, o**r**ange ca**rr**ot. He had hidden it unde**r** a **r**eally big **r**ock. **R**ick turned the **r**ock ove**r**…

The o**r**ange ca**rr**ot was gone!

"**R-r-r-r-r-r-r-r-r-r**! Someone has **r**obbed me!" **r**oared **R**ick.
He was ve**r**y angry. "I will find this **r**obbe**r**!"

Rick saw **R**andy the gi**r**affe, **r**eaching up to eat the leaves from a tree. Maybe **R**andy had taken his ca**rr**ot!

"**R**andy! Did you take my ca**rr**ot? Is it up the**r**e, in your tree?" said **R**ick.

"No, **R**ick. I didn't take you**r** ca**rr**ot. You could ask Te**rr**y the pa**rr**ot," said **R**andy.

Te**rr**y was **r**esting on the **r**oof of his cage.

"Te**rr**y, did you take my ca**rr**ot and hide it in you**r** cage?" asked **R**ick.

"No, I didn't take you**r** ca**rr**ot," said Te**rr**y. "Try asking **R**ebecca the alligato**r**."

Rebecca was **r**elaxing in the **r**ive**r**.

"**R**ebecca, did you take my ca**rr**ot?" **R**ick asked. He was a bit scared – **R**ebecca was an alligato**r** afte**r** all.

"Why don't you look inside my mouth and see?" said **R**ebecca with a **r**umble, and opened he**r** mouth **r**eally wide. He**r** teeth we**r**e **r**eally sharp looking!

"That's all **r**ight, I'll just go," said **R**ick and **r**an away as fast as he could.

Rick **r**an back to his **r**ock, feeling sad. On his way, he spotted something o**r**ange and ve**r**y **r**ipe looking …

It was next to a pile of **r**ed che**rr**ies and someone was eating it …

… it was **R**alph the **r**at!

"**R**alph! You took my ca**rr**ot!" said **R**ick.

"Oh, this was you**r** ca**rr**ot. I didn't **r**ealise," said **R**alph. Half the ca**rr**ot was already gone.

"I'm **r**eally so**rr**y, **R**ick. You can have the **r**est of the ca**rr**ot, and some of my che**rr**ies to make up fo**r** it," said **R**alph.

"Well, that would be nice," said **R**ick.

So **R**ick the **r**abbit and **R**alph the **r**obber-**r**at ate the **r**est of the o**r**ange ca**rr**ot and the **r**ed che**rr**ies togethe**r**.

"It's nice to sha**r**e," said **R**ick.